Contents

CW00408308

Euro 2000 – page 4
Starting XI Germany 2001 – page 5
World Cup 2002 – page 6
First Goals – page 9
Euro 2004 – page 11
World Cup 2006 – page 13
Euro 2008 – page 15
Legends and One Cap Wonders – page 16
World Cup 2010 – page 18
Starting XI versus Germany 2010 – page 20
Red Cards – page 21
Euro 2012 – page 24
Friendlies – page 26
World Cup 2014 – page 29
Euro 2016 – page 31
Starting XI versus Iceland – page 34
First Goals II – page 35
World Cup 2018 – page 37
Starting XI versus Colombia – page 40
Legends and One Cap Wonders II – page 41
Euro 2020 – page 43
Nations League – page 45
Managers – page 46

Euro 2000 Answers – page 48

Starting XI Germany 2001 Answers – page 50

World Cup 2002 Answers – page 51

First Goals Answers – page 55

Euro 2004 Answers – page 58

World Cup 2006 Answers – page 62

Euro 2008 Answers – page 66

Legends and One Cap Wonders Answers – page 68

World Cup 2010 Answers – page 70

Starting XI versus Germany 2010 Answers – page 74

Red Cards Answers – page 75

Euro 2012 Answers – page 77

Friendlies Answers – page 81

World Cup 2014 Answers – page 84

Euro 2016 Answers – page 87

Starting XI versus Iceland Answers – page 90

First Goals II Answers – page 91

World Cup 2018 Answers – page 93

Starting XI versus Colombia Answers – page 98

Legends and One Cap Wonders II Answers – page 99

Euro 2020 Answers – page 102

Nations League Answers – page 104

Managers Answers – page 106

Euro 2000

1) Who was the England manager during the Euro 2000 tournament?

2) Who put England 1-0 up inside the first three minutes of their Euro 2000 opening game against Portugal?

3) England lost their groups games against both Portugal and Romania by what score-line?

4) Who scored the only goal as England beat Germany in their second group match?

5) Which player conceded the late penalty against Romania which saw England knocked out of Euro 2000 in the group stage?

Starting XI versus Germany 2001

Can you name the England starting line-up from their 5-1 win over Germany in 2001 from the initials provided?

D.S

G.N

R.F

S.C

A.C

N.B

P.S

S.G

D.B

E.H

M.O

World Cup 2002 Qualifying

1) England lost the final ever game at the old Wembley Stadium as which German player scored the only goal of the game?

2) England picked up their first win in qualifying with a 2-1 home win over Finland at which stadium?

3) Albania were beaten 3-1 away from home in March 2001, which player scored his only international goal deep into stoppage time to secure the points?

4) England famously beat Germany 5-1 in September 2001, which three players scored for England in the match?

5) Which player had put Germany 1-0 in the same game?

6) David Beckham scored his legendary last-minute free kick against Greece to send England to the 2002 World Cup, but which other England player came on as a substitute and scored with his first touch in the match?

World Cup 2002 Tournament

1) Who scored England's goal as they went ahead against Sweden in their opening game?

2) What was the final score in that group stage match?

3) Which future Premier League manager was penalised for the foul on Michael Owen which gave David Beckham the chance to score from spot, securing a 1-0 win over Argentina in the group stage match?

4) Who opened the scoring as England beat Denmark 3-0 in their Round of 16 meeting?

5) Brazil knocked England out at the Quarter Final stage with a 2-1 win, but which Brazilian was sent off in the game?

First Goals

1) Who scored with his first touch in international football to seal a 3-2 win over Scotland in 2013?

2) Who scored within the first five minutes of his England debut in a World Cup warm up match against Australia in 2016?

3) Who did Steven Gerrard score his first England goal against?

4) Francis Jeffers scored on his only international appearance in a friendly against who in February 2003?

5) Jamie Vardy scored his first England goal in a friendly against which Country in March 2016?

6) Who scored on his only England appearance in the Euro 2008 qualifier against Andorra?

7) Frank Lampard scored his first England goal on his 12th appearance, against which team did he break his duck?

8) Wayne Rooney scored his first England goal against which team?

9) Which player scored twice on his international debut in a friendly against the USA in May 2005?

10) Harry Kane scored within two minutes of coming on as a substitute on his England debut against which team?

Euro 2004 Qualifying

1) England came from behind to beat Slovakia 2-1 away from home in their first qualifier for Euro 2004 thanks to goals from which two players?

2) Which long-serving goalkeeper made his last international appearance in the 2-2 draw with Macedonia in October 2002?

3) At which ground did England beat Turkey in their home qualifier in April 2003?

4) Which team did England beat 2-1 at the Riverside Stadium in June 2003?

5) Who blazed his penalty over the bar in the 0-0 draw away in Turkey, a result which guaranteed promotion to Euro 2004?

Euro 2004 Tournament

1) Which French player scored twice in stoppage time as England collapsed to a 2-1 defeat in their opening game?

2) Which side did England beat 3-0 in their second group game?

3) England sealed qualification for the knock-out rounds by beating Croatia by what score?

4) Portugal ultimately knocked England out on Penalties in the Quarter Finals, but who had put England in front after just 3 minutes?

5) Which two England players missed penalties in the shoot-out as England lost 6-5?

World Cup 2006 Qualifying

1) England beat Wales at home by what score-line?

2) At which Premier League ground did England beat Azerbaijan 2-0 in March 2005?

3) Who scored the only goal as England beat Wales at the Millennium Stadium in September 2005?

4) Which Northern Ireland player scored the goal that beat England at Windsor Park in September 2005?

5) England secured top place in the group with a 2-1 win over which team in the last qualifying game?

6) Who was England's top scorer during qualification with five goals?

World Cup 2006 Tournament

1) Against which country did Joe Cole score his spectacular dipping volley in the 2006 World Cup?

2) Who did England play in their opening game of the 2006 World Cup?

3) Which two players scored the late goals as England struggled to a 2-0 win over Trinidad and Tobago in their second group match?

4) Which Swedish player scored a late equaliser in the final group stage game as the match ended 2-2?

5) Who scored the only goal as England beat Ecuador 1-0 in the Round of 16?

6) In the 2006 World Cup Quarter Final against Portugal, which three players missed penalties for England?

Euro 2008 Qualifying

1) England began their Euro 2008 qualifying campaign with a 5-0 win over which team?

2) Who scored an own-goal as Croatia beat England 2-0 in October 2006?

3) Which Russian player scored twice as England threw away a lead to lose 2-1 in Moscow in October 2007?

4) England failed to qualify for Euro 2008 after losing their last qualifying game at home to Croatia by what score?

5) England finished third in their qualifying group, which team did they finish just above due to the head-to-head record between the two sides?

6) Michael Owen's last international goals came in a Euro 2008 qualifier against which country in September 2007?

Legends and One Cap Wonders

1) Alan Shearer scored in his final international appearance against which country in the year 2000?

2) Which Leeds central midfielder won his only cap against Portugal in September 2002?

3) Which forward made his final England appearance at the age of 36 in the 2002 World Cup against Brazil?

4) Michael Ball and Gavin McCann both won their only caps in a friendly against which side at Villa Park in February 2001?

5) Which player, who would go on to win over 100 caps, made his debut against Ukraine in May 2000?

6) David Beckham won his 115th and last cap against which team in 2009?

7) Against which Country did David Beckham win his 100th cap in 2008?

8) Which young Derby County midfielder made his only England appearance against Italy in November 2000?

World Cup 2010 Qualifying

1) Who scored a brace as England began their campaign with a 2-0 win in Andorra?

2) Who scored a hat-trick as England beat Croatia 4-1 away from home in September 2008?

3) Which team did England beat 6-0 at Wembley in June 2009?

4) By what score-line did England beat Croatia at home towards the end of the qualifying campaign?

5) Which team inflicted the only defeat on England in their qualification group?

6) Which England player was the top scorer in their qualifying group with 9 goals?

World Cup 2010 Tournament

1) Who scored England's goal in their 1-1 draw with the USA in their opening Group game?

2) Who was the goalkeeper who infamously let Clint Dempsey's shot squirm passed him to allow the USA to equalise in that match?

3) Which player scored the only goal against Slovenia in the final Group Stage match to see England qualify for the Knock-out round?

4) During the 4-1 defeat to Germany in their Round of 16 meeting, which England player hit the shot which went over the line, but was not given as a goal?

5) Who scored England's only goal in that match?

Starting XI versus Germany 2010

Can you name the England starting line-up from their 4-1 defeat to Germany in the 2010 World Cup from the initials provided?

D.J

G.J

A.C

J.T

M.U

S.G

F.L

G.B

J.M

W.R

J.D

Red Cards

1) Who was sent off for picking up two bookings during England's disappointing 2-2 draw at home to Macedonia in October 2002?

2) Which player became the first to receive two red cards in their England career when they were dismissed against Austria in October 2005?

3) Wayne Rooney was sent off in the 2006 World Cup for stamping on which Portuguese player?

4) Who was the first ever goalkeeper to be sent off whilst playing for England in 2009?

5) Wayne Rooney missed the start of Euro 2012 through suspension after being sent off in the final qualification game against which country?

6) Who was dismissed in the World Cup qualifying draw against Ukraine in September 2012?

7) Raheem Sterling was sent off during a fiery friendly game against which country in a warm-up before the 2014 World Cup?

Euro 2012 Qualifying

1) England began their qualifying campaign with a 4-0 home win over Bulgaria, who scored a hat-trick in the game?

2) Wales were beaten 2-0 at the Millennium Stadium in March 2011, which two England players scored the goals in the opening 15 minutes?

3) England won 3-0 away from home against Bulgaria in September 2011, Wayne Rooney scored twice, but which centre-back opened the scoring?

4) What was the score in the home fixture against Wales in September 2011?

5) Which team qualified for the Play-offs by finishing second behind England in the group?

Euro 2012 Tournament

1) Who was the England goalkeeper throughout the Euro 2012 tournament?

2) Who scored England's goal in the 1-1 draw with France in their opening Group Stage game?

3) By what score did England beat Sweden in their second match of the tournament?

4) In the 1-0 win over Ukraine, which England defender cleared a shot off the line, only for replays to show the ball may have crossed the line?

5) England lost to Italy on penalties in the Quarter-Finals, which two England players missed in the shoot-out?

Friendlies

1) Who headed home the late winner to hand England a 3-2 win away to Germany in March 2016?

2) Who chipped his penalty over the bar during the 6-0 win over Jamaica in 2006, although he did later complete his hat-trick?

3) Which team did England beat 6-1 in a Euro 2004 warm-up match?

4) England suffered a demoralising 4-1 loss away to which country in August 2005?

5) Who scored twice late on to hand England a memorable 3-2 victory over Argentina in November 2005?

6) England scored in stoppage time, only to then concede a minute later to lose a dramatic match 3-2 against which side at Wembley in February 2012?

7) Sweden opened their new stadium with a 4-2 victory over England in 2012, which Swedish player grabbed all four goals for his country?

8) With Gareth Southgate still in temporary charge of England, he saw his team concede twice very late on to draw 2-2 with which team in 2016?

9) England drew 0-0 against which two teams within the same week in November 2017?

10) Where did England play their 2018 World Cup warm-up match against Costa Rica, which they won 2-0?

11) Who was made captain for the friendly with the USA in 2018?

12) Paul Scholes hit a trademark long-range effort from 30 yards in a friendly against which country in May 2001 at Pride Park?

13) Frank Lampard scored his last international goal in a friendly against which team in May 2013?

14) Who scored an own-goal with a diving header against Australia in May 2016?

World Cup 2014 Qualifying

1) England beat Moldova 5-0 away from home in their opening qualifying match, which full-back scored the only goal of his international career to finish off the scoring?

2) Who scored the late penalty as England rescued a point at home to Ukraine in September 2012?

3) By what score-line did England beat San Marino away from home in March 2013?

4) England secured qualification by beating Poland 2-0 at home in the last match, which two players scored that day?

5) Which team did England finish one point ahead of to win their qualifying group?

6) How many games did England lose in their qualification group?

World Cup 2014 Tournament

1) Who scored England's goal in their 2-1 loss to Italy in their opening group game?

2) England were eliminated after losing 2-1 to Uruguay, who scored both goals for their opponents?

3) Who started in goal for England in their final match against Costa Rica?

4) England ultimately finished bottom of their group, but which team finished top?

Euro 2016 Qualifying

1) Who scored a brace as England began their campaign with a 2-0 win away against Switzerland?

2) Who opened the scoring in the 5-0 home win over San Marino in October 2014?

3) England fell behind at home to Slovenia before coming back to win 3-1, but which player had scored an own goal to put the Slovenian's ahead?

4) Jack Wilshere scored a spectacular brace as England secured an entertaining 3-2 away win against which opponents in June 2015?

5) How many goals did England concede in their 10 qualification games?

6) Wayne Rooney broke Bobby Charlton's England goal-scoring record by hitting his 50th international goal against which country?

Euro 2016 Tournament

1) Who scored the free-kick which gave England the lead in their opening game against Russia?

2) Who scored the stoppage time winner as England beat Wales 2-1 in the group stage?

3) What was the score in England's final group match against Slovakia?

4) In what position did England finish in their group?

5) England crashed out to Iceland in the Round of 16 with a 2-1 defeat, but who had won the penalty that gave England the lead in the match?

Starting XI versus Iceland

Can you name the England starting line-up from their 2-1 defeat to Iceland in Euro 2016 from the initials provided?

J.H
K.W
G.C
C.S
D.R
D.A
E.D
W.R
D.S
H.K
R.S

First Goals II

1) Which Manchester City winger scored on his debut against Ukraine at St James' Park in 2004?

2) Who did Tammy Abraham score his first international goal against?

3) Which Aston Villa striker scored against the Netherlands on his debut in 2002?

4) Which Tottenham winger scored in England's 4-1 win over Montenegro in October 2013?

5) Which centre-back scored during his only game for England in the 4-2 friendly loss to Sweden in November 2013?

6) Callum Wilson scored on his debut versus which Country in November 2018?

7) Mason Mount scored his first goal for England in an away match against which Country in November 2019?

World Cup 2018 Qualifying

1) Who scored the winner deep into second-half stoppage time to give England a 1-0 win away to Slovakia in their opening qualification game?

2) Who scored his final international goal in the 2-0 win over Lithuania in March 2017?

3) Which Scottish player scored two late free-kicks during the 2-2 draw at Hampden Park in June 2017?

4) England were only 1-0 up away against Malta with 85 minutes gone, but what was the final score?

5) England only dropped points in two qualification games with draws against Scotland and which other team?

World Cup 2018 Tournament

1) What was the score as England beat Tunisia in their opening game?

2) Who opened the scoring in England's 6-1 win over Panama in the 2018 World Cup?

3) Who scored a beautiful curled effort into the top corner from the edge of the box against Panama in the 2018 World Cup?

4) Who captained England in their final group match against Belgium, as both teams rested players having already qualified for the knockout rounds?

5) England beat Columbia on penalties in their Round of 16 match, but who was the only England player to miss his spot-kick?

6) Which England player won the man of the match award for their performance in the 2-0 win over Sweden in the Quarter-Finals?

7) Who scored the free-kick which put England ahead in their Semi-Final against Croatia?

8) What was the score in the Third Place Play-Off against Belgium?

9) How many of Harry Kane's goals in the tournament came from the penalty spot?

10) How many goals did Harry Kane score as he won the Golden Boot award?

Starting XI versus Colombia

Can you name the England starting line-up from their World Cup 2018 Second Round match with Colombia from the initials provided?

J.P

K.W

J.S

H.M

J.H

K.T

J.L

D.A

A.Y

R.S

H.K

Legends and One Cap Wonders II

1) Frank Lampard won his final international cap in the 2014 World Cup against which Country?

2) Which controversial midfielder won his only cap against Spain in 2007?

3) Which player retired with 107 caps to his name just before the 2014 World Cup Finals?

4) Which Bolton player appeared once for England, against Montenegro in October 2010?

5) Which player, who debuted against Australia in 2003, won 8 caps before his 18th birthday?

6) Which striker made his debut against Trinidad & Tobago in 2008 before having his career ended by injury?

7) Which goalkeeper won his only cap against Italy in August 2012?

8) Against which country did Wayne Rooney make his farewell appearance in 2018?

9) Who made two appearances for England, in 2012 and 2013, before switching to play for the Ivory Coast?

Euro 2020 Qualifying

1) Which player scored a hat-trick in the victory over the Czech Republic in the opening group match?

2) Who scored a brace in the 5-1 win away against Montenegro?

3) What was the score as England beat Kosovo in an entertaining encounter at St Mary's?

4) England dropped points in only one game when they lost away from home to which side?

5) By what score did England beat Bulgaria away from home?

6) Montenegro were hammered at Wembley by what score-line in November 2019?

7) Harry Kane was the top scorer in the group with how many goals?

Nations League

1) England won their Nations League group despite having how many points after the first two games?

2) What was the score as England claimed an impressive victory away from home against Spain?

3) Which two players scored the late goals as England came from behind to beat Croatia 2-1 to win the group?

4) England were beaten by the Netherlands in extra-time of their Semi-Final, which England player scored an own-goal during the added period?

5) England beat Switzerland 6-5 on penalties to secure a win in the third place play-off, who was the unlikely scorer of England's fifth penalty in the shoot-out?

Managers

1) Which match was the last that Kevin Keegan managed the England team?

2) Who was caretaker manager for England's 0-0 draw away to Finland in October 2000?

3) Which manager was the first to hand David Beckham the captaincy of England, doing so in a friendly versus Italy in 2000?

4) How many major Quarter-Finals did Sven-Goran Eriksson lead England to?

5) Who was England manager when they drew 1-1 with Brazil in the first game at the new Wembley Stadium in June 2007?

6) Fabio Capello left his role as England manager in 2012, with his final game being a 1-0 win over who in November 2011?

7) Who took charge of England for their 3-2 friendly defeat to the Netherlands in February 2012?

8) Who did Roy Hodgson make permanent captain of England shortly after he took control as manager?

9) Sam Allardyce famously only managed England for one match, a late win against which team?

10) Gareth Southgate faced Germany in his first match after being confirmed as permanent England manager in 2017, but who captained the side that day?

11) Which manager had taken charge of England on the most occasions this century?

Answers

Euro 2000 – Answers

1) Who was the England manager during the Euro 2000 tournament?
Kevin Keegan

2) Who put England 1-0 up inside the first three minutes of their Euro 2000 opening game against Portugal?
Paul Scholes

3) England lost their groups games against both Portugal and Romania by what score-line?
3-2

4) Who scored the only goal as England beat Germany in their second group match?
Alan Shearer

5) Which player conceded the late penalty against Romania which saw England knocked out of Euro 2000 in the group stage?
Phil Neville

Starting XI versus Germany 2001 – Answers

Can you name the England starting line-up from their 5-1 win over Germany in 2001 from the initials provided?

David Seaman
Gary Neville
Rio Ferdinand
Sol Campbell
Ashley Cole
Nick Barmby
Paul Scholes
Steven Gerrard
David Beckham
Emile Heskey
Michael Owen

World Cup 2002 Qualifying – Answers

1) England lost the final ever game at the old Wembley Stadium as which German player scored the only goal of the game?
Dietmar Hamann

2) England picked up their first win in qualifying with a 2-1 home win over Finland at which stadium?
Anfield

3) Albania were beaten 3-1 away from home in March 2001, which player scored his only international goal deep into stoppage time to secure the points?
Andy Cole

4) England famously beat Germany 5-1 in September 2001, which three players scored for England in the match?
Michael Owen, Steven Gerrard and Emile Heskey

5) Which player had put Germany 1-0 in the same game?

Carsten Jancker

6) David Beckham scored his legendary last-minute free kick against Greece to send England to the 2002 World Cup, but which other England player came on as a substitute and scored with his first touch in the match?

Teddy Sheringham

World Cup 2002 Tournament – Answers

1) Who scored England's goal as they went ahead against Sweden in their opening game?
   Sol Campbell

2) What was the final score in that group stage match?
   1-1

3) Which future Premier League manager was penalised for the foul on Michael Owen which gave David Beckham the chance to score from spot, securing a 1-0 win over Argentina in the group stage match?
   Mauricio Pochettino

4) Who opened the scoring as England beat Denmark 3-0 in their Round of 16 meeting?
   Rio Ferdinand

5) Brazil knocked England out at the Quarter Final stage with a 2-1 win, but which Brazilian was sent off in the game?
Ronaldinho

First Goals – Answers

1) Who scored with his first touch in international football to seal a 3-2 win over Scotland in 2013?
   Rickie Lambert

2) Who scored within the first five minutes of his England debut in a World Cup warm up match against Australia in 2016?
   Marcus Rashford

3) Who did Steven Gerrard score his first England goal against?
   Germany

4) Francis Jeffers scored on his only international appearance in a friendly against who in February 2003?
   Australia

5) Jamie Vardy scored his first England goal in a friendly against which Country in March 2016?
Germany

6) Who scored on his only England appearance in the Euro 2008 qualifier against Andorra?
David Nugent

7) Frank Lampard scored his first England goal on his 12th appearance, against which team did he break his duck?
Croatia

8) Wayne Rooney scored his first England goal against which team?
Macedonia

9) Which player scored twice on his international debut in a friendly against the USA in May 2005?
Kieran Richardson

10) Harry Kane scored within two minutes of coming on as a substitute on his England debut against which team?
Lithuania

Euro 2004 Qualifying – Answers

1) England came from behind to beat Slovakia 2-1 away from home in their first qualifier for Euro 2004 thanks to goals from which two players?
David Beckham and Michael Owen

2) Which long-serving goalkeeper made his last international appearance in the 2-2 draw with Macedonia in October 2002?
David Seaman

3) At which ground did England beat Turkey in their home qualifier in April 2003?
The Stadium of Light – Sunderland

4) Which team did England beat 2-1 at the Riverside Stadium in June 2003?
Slovakia

5) Who blazed his penalty over the bar in the 0-0 draw away in Turkey, a result which guaranteed promotion to Euro 2004?
David Beckham

Euro 2004 Tournament – Answers

1) Which French player scored twice in stoppage time as England collapsed to a 2-1 defeat in their opening game?
Zinedine Zidane

2) Which side did England beat 3-0 in their second group game?
Switzerland

3) England sealed qualification for the knock-out rounds by beating Croatia by what score?
4-2

4) Portugal ultimately knocked England out on Penalties in the Quarter Finals, but who had put England in front after just 3 minutes?
Michael Owen

5) Which two England players missed penalties in the shoot-out as England lost 6-5?

Darius Vassell

World Cup 2006 Qualifying – Answers

1) England beat Wales at home by what score-line?
   2-0

2) At which Premier League ground did England beat Azerbaijan 2-0 in March 2005?
   St James' Park

3) Who scored the only goal as England beat Wales at the Millennium Stadium in September 2005?
   Joe Cole

4) Which Northern Ireland player scored the goal that beat England at Windsor Park in September 2005?
   David Healy

5) England secured top place in the group with a 2-1 win over which team in the last qualifying game?
   Poland

6) Who was England's top scorer during qualification with five goals?
Frank Lampard

World Cup 2006 Tournament – Answers

1) Against which country did Joe Cole score his spectacular dipping volley in the 2006 World Cup?
Sweden

2) Who did England play in their opening game of the 2006 World Cup?
Paraguay

3) Which two players scored the late goals as England struggled to a 2-0 win over Trinidad and Tobago in their second group match?
Peter Crouch and Steven Gerrard

4) Which Swedish player scored a late equaliser in the final group stage game as the match ended 2-2?
Henrik Larsson

5) Who scored the only goal as England beat Ecuador 1-0 in the Round of 16?
David Beckham

6) In the 2006 World Cup Quarter Final against Portugal, which three players missed penalties for England?
Frank Lampard, Steven Gerrard and Jamie Carragher

Euro 2008 Qualifying – Answers

1) England began their Euro 2008 qualifying campaign with a 5-0 win over which team?
Andorra

2) Who scored an own-goal as Croatia beat England 2-0 in October 2006?
Gary Neville

3) Which Russian player scored twice as England threw away a lead to lose 2-1 in Moscow in October 2007?
Roman Pavlyuchenko

4) England failed to qualify for Euro 2008 after losing their last qualifying game at home to Croatia by what score?
3-2

5) England finished third in their qualifying group, which team did they finish just above due to the head-to-head record between the two sides?
Israel

6) Michael Owen's last international goals came in a Euro 2008 qualifier against which country in September 2007?
Russia

**Legends and One Cap Wonders –
Answers**

1) Alan Shearer scored in his final
   international appearance against which
   country in the year 2000?
   Romania

2) Which Leeds central midfielder won his
   only cap against Portugal in September
   2002?
   Lee Bowyer

3) Which forward made his final England
   appearance at the age of 36 in the 2002
   World Cup against Brazil?
   Teddy Sheringham

4) Michael Ball and Gavin McCann both
   won their only caps in a friendly against
   which side at Villa Park in February
   2001?
   Spain

5) Which player, who would go on to win over 100 caps, made his debut against Ukraine in May 2000?
Steven Gerrard

6) David Beckham won his 115th and last cap against which team in 2009?
Belarus

7) Against which Country did David Beckham win his 100th cap in 2008?
France

8) Which young Derby County midfielder made his only England appearance against Italy in November 2000?
Seth Johnson

World Cup 2010 Qualifying – Answers

1) Who scored a brace as England began their campaign with a 2-0 win in Andorra?
Joe Cole

2) Who scored a hat-trick as England beat Croatia 4-1 away from home in September 2008?
Theo Walcott

3) Which team did England beat 6-0 at Wembley in June 2009?
Andorra

4) By what score-line did England beat Croatia at home towards the end of the qualifying campaign?
5-1

5) Which team inflicted the only defeat on England in their qualification group?
Ukraine

6) Which England player was the top scorer in their qualifying group with 9 goals?
Wayne Rooney

World Cup 2010 Tournament – Answers

1) Who scored England's goal in their 1-1 draw with the USA in their opening Group game?
Steven Gerrard

2) Who was the goalkeeper who infamously let Clint Dempsey's shot squirm passed him to allow the USA to equalise in that match?
Rob Green

3) Which player scored the only goal against Slovenia in the final Group Stage match to see England qualify for the Knock-out round?
Jermain Defoe

4) During the 4-1 defeat to Germany in their Round of 16 meeting, which England player hit the shot which went over the line, but was not given as a goal?
Frank Lampard

5) Who scored England's only goal in that match?
Matthew Upson

Starting XI versus Germany 2010 – Answers

Can you name the England starting line-up from their 4-1 defeat to Germany in the 2010 World Cup from the initials provided?

David James
Glen Johnson
Ashley Cole
John Terry
Matthew Upson
Steven Gerrard
Frank Lampard
Gareth Barry
James Milner
Wayne Rooney
Jermain Defoe

Red Cards – Answers

1) Who was sent off for picking up two bookings during England's disappointing 2-2 draw at home to Macedonia in October 2002?
Alan Smith

2) Which player became the first to receive two red cards in their England career when they were dismissed against Austria in October 2005?
David Beckham

3) Wayne Rooney was sent off in the 2006 World Cup for stamping on which Portuguese player?
Ricardo Carvalho

4) Who was the first ever goalkeeper to be sent off whilst playing for England in 2009?
Rob Green

5) Wayne Rooney missed the start of Euro 2012 through suspension after being sent off in the final qualification game against which country?
Montenegro

6) Who was dismissed in the World Cup qualifying draw against Ukraine in September 2012?
Steven Gerrard

7) Raheem Sterling was sent off during a fiery friendly game against which country in a warm-up before the 2014 World Cup?
Ecuador

Euro 2012 Qualifying – Answers

1) England began their qualifying campaign with a 4-0 home win over Bulgaria, who scored a hat-trick in the game?
Jermain Defoe

2) Wales were beaten 2-0 at the Millennium Stadium in March 2011, which two England players scored the goals in the opening 15 minutes?
Frank Lampard and Darren Bent

3) England won 3-0 away from home against Bulgaria in September 2011, Wayne Rooney scored twice, but which centre-back opened the scoring?
Gary Cahill

4) What was the score in the home fixture against Wales in September 2011?
England 1-0 Wales

5) Which team qualified for the Play-offs by finishing second behind England in the group?

Montenegro

Euro 2012 Tournament – Answers

1) Who was the England goalkeeper throughout the Euro 2012 tournament?
Joe Hart

2) Who scored England's goal in the 1-1 draw with France in their opening Group Stage game?
Joleon Lescott

3) By what score did England beat Sweden in their second match of the tournament?
3-2

4) In the 1-0 win over Ukraine, which England defender cleared a shot off the line, only for replays to show the ball may have crossed the line?
John Terry

5) England lost to Italy on penalties in the Quarter-Finals, which two England players missed in the shoot-out?
Ashley Young and Ashley Cole

Friendlies – Answers

1) Who headed home the late winner to hand England a 3-2 win away to Germany in March 2016?
Eric Dier

2) Who chipped his penalty over the bar during the 6-0 win over Jamaica in 2006, although he did later complete his hat-trick?
Peter Crouch

3) Which team did England beat 6-1 in a Euro 2004 warm-up match?
Iceland

4) England suffered a demoralising 4-1 loss away to which country in August 2005?
Denmark

5) Who scored twice late on to hand England a memorable 3-2 victory over Argentina in November 2005?
Michael Owen

6) England scored in stoppage time, only to then concede a minute later to lose a dramatic match 3-2 against which side at Wembley in February 2012?
Netherlands

7) Sweden opened their new stadium with a 4-2 victory over England in 2012, which Swedish player grabbed all four goals for his country?
Zlatan Ibrahimovic

8) With Gareth Southgate still in temporary charge of England, he saw his team concede twice very late on to draw 2-2 with which team in 2016?
Spain

9) England drew 0-0 against which two teams within the same week in November 2017?
Germany and Brazil

10) Where did England play their 2018 World Cup warm-up match against Costa Rica, which they won 2-0?
Elland Road

11) Who was made captain for the friendly with the USA in 2018?
Fabian Delph

12) Paul Scholes hit a trademark long-range effort from 30 yards in a friendly against which country in May 2001 at Pride Park?
Mexico

13) Frank Lampard scored his last international goal in a friendly against which team in May 2013?
Republic of Ireland

14) Who scored an own-goal with a diving header against Australia in May 2016?
Eric Dier

World Cup 2014 Qualifying – Answers

1) England beat Moldova 5-0 away from home in their opening qualifying match, which full-back scored the only goal of his international career to finish off the scoring?
Leighton Baines

2) Who scored the late penalty as England rescued a point at home to Ukraine in September 2012?
Frank Lampard

3) By what score-line did England beat San Marino away from home in March 2013?
8-0

4) England secured qualification by beating Poland 2-0 at home in the last match, which two players scored that day?
Wayne Rooney and Steven Gerrard

5) Which team did England finish one point ahead of to win their qualifying group?
Ukraine

6) How many games did England lose in their qualification group?
None

World Cup 2014 Tournament – Answers

1) Who scored England's goal in their 2-1 loss to Italy in their opening group game?
Daniel Sturridge

2) England were eliminated after losing 2-1 to Uruguay, who scored both goals for their opponents?
Luis Suarez

3) Who started in goal for England in their final match against Costa Rica?
Ben Foster

4) England ultimately finished bottom of their group, but which team finished top?
Costa Rica

Euro 2016 Qualifying – Answers

1) Who scored a brace as England began their campaign with a 2-0 win away against Switzerland?
Danny Welbeck

2) Who opened the scoring in the 5-0 home win over San Marino in October 2014?
Phil Jagielka

3) England fell behind at home to Slovenia before coming back to win 3-1, but which player had scored an own goal to put the Slovenian's ahead?
Jordan Henderson

4) Jack Wilshere scored a spectacular brace as England secured an entertaining 3-2 away win against which opponents in June 2015?
Slovenia

5) How many goals did England concede in their 10 qualification games?
Three

6) Wayne Rooney broke Bobby Charlton's England goal-scoring record by hitting his 50th international goal against which country?
Switzerland

Euro 2016 Tournament – Answers

1) Who scored the free-kick which gave England the lead in their opening game against Russia?
Eric Dier

2) Who scored the stoppage time winner as England beat Wales 2-1 in the group stage?
Daniel Sturridge

3) What was the score in England's final group match against Slovakia?
0-0

4) In what position did England finish in their group?
Second

5) England crashed out to Iceland in the Round of 16 with a 2-1 defeat, but who had won the penalty that gave England the lead in the match?
Raheem Sterling

Starting XI versus Iceland – Answers

Can you name the England starting line-up from their 2-1 defeat to Iceland in Euro 2016 from the initials provided?

Joe Hart
Kyle Walker
Gary Cahill
Chris Smalling
Danny Rose
Dele Alli
Eric Dier
Wayne Rooney
Daniel Sturridge
Harry Kane
Raheem Sterling

First Goals II – Answers

1) Which Manchester City winger scored on his debut against Ukraine at St James' Park in 2004?
Shaun Wright-Phillips

2) Who did Tammy Abraham score his first international goal against?
Montenegro

3) Which Aston Villa striker scored against the Netherlands on his debut in 2002?
Darius Vassell

4) Which Tottenham winger scored in England's 4-1 win over Montenegro in October 2013?
Andros Townsend

5) Which centre-back scored during his only game for England in the 4-2 friendly loss to Sweden in November 2013?
Steven Caulker

6) Callum Wilson scored on his debut versus which Country in November 2018?
USA

7) Mason Mount scored his first goal for England in an away match against which Country in November 2019?
Kosovo

World Cup 2018 Qualifying – Answers

1) Who scored the winner deep into second-half stoppage time to give England a 1-0 win away to Slovakia in their opening qualification game?
Adam Lallana

2) Who scored his final international goal in the 2-0 win over Lithuania in March 2017?
Jermain Defoe

3) Which Scottish player scored two late free-kicks during the 2-2 draw at Hampden Park in June 2017?
Leigh Griffiths

4) England were only 1-0 up away against Malta with 85 minutes gone, but what was the final score?
4-0

5) England only dropped points in two qualification games with draws against Scotland and which other team?
Slovenia

World Cup 2018 Tournament – Answers

1) What was the score as England beat Tunisia in their opening game?
2-1

2) Who opened the scoring in England's 6-1 win over Panama in the 2018 World Cup?
John Stones

3) Who scored a beautiful curled effort into the top corner from the edge of the box against Panama in the 2018 World Cup?
Jesse Lingard

4) Who captained England in their final group match against Belgium, as both teams rested players having already qualified for the knockout rounds?
Eric Dier

5) England beat Columbia on penalties in their Round of 16 match, but who was the only England player to miss his spot-kick?
Jordan Henderson

6) Which England player won the man of the match award for their performance in the 2-0 win over Sweden in the Quarter-Finals?
Jordan Pickford

7) Who scored the free-kick which put England ahead in their Semi-Final against Croatia?
Kieran Trippier

8) What was the score in the Third Place Play-Off against Belgium?
Belgium 2-0 England

9) How many of Harry Kane's goals in the tournament came from the penalty spot?
Three

10) How many goals did Harry Kane score as he won the Golden Boot award?

Six

Starting XI versus Colombia - Answers

Can you name the England starting line-up from their World Cup 2018 Second Round match with Colombia from the initials provided?

Jordan Pickford
Kyle Walker
John Stones
Harry Maguire
Jordan Henderson
Kieran Trippier
Jesse Lingard
Dele Alli
Ashley Young
Raheem Sterling
Harry Kane

**Legends and One Cap Wonders II –
Answers**

1) Frank Lampard won his final
   international cap in the 2014 World Cup
   against which Country?
   Costa Rica

2) Which controversial midfielder won his
   only cap against Spain in 2007?
   Joey Barton

3) Which player retired with 107 caps to his
   name just before the 2014 World Cup
   Finals?
   Ashley Cole

4) Which Bolton player appeared once for
   England, against Montenegro in October
   2010?
   Kevin Davies

5) Which player, who debuted against Australia in 2003, won 8 caps before his 18th birthday?
Wayne Rooney

6) Which striker made his debut against Trinidad & Tobago in 2008 before having his career ended by injury?
Dean Ashton

7) Which goalkeeper won his only cap against Italy in August 2012?
John Ruddy

8) Against which country did Wayne Rooney make his farewell appearance in 2018?
USA

9) Who made two appearances for England, in 2012 and 2013, before switching to play for the Ivory Coast?
Wilfried Zaha

Euro 2020 Qualifying – Answers

1) Which player scored a hat-trick in the victory over the Czech Republic in the opening group match?
Raheem Sterling

2) Who scored a brace in the 5-1 win away against Montenegro?
Ross Barkley

3) What was the score as England beat Kosovo in an entertaining encounter at St Mary's?
5-3

4) England dropped points in only one game when they lost away from home to which side?
Czech Republic

5) By what score did England beat Bulgaria away from home?
6-0

6) Montenegro were hammered at Wembley by what score-line in November 2019?

7-0

7) Harry Kane was the top scorer in the group with how many goals?

12

Nations League – Answers

1) England won their Nations League group despite having how many points after the first two games?
One

2) What was the score as England claimed an impressive victory away from home against Spain?
3-2

3) Which two players scored the late goals as England came from behind to beat Croatia 2-1 to win the group?
Jesse Lingard and Harry Kane

4) England were beaten by the Netherlands in extra-time of their Semi-Final, which England player scored an own-goal during the added period?
Kyle Walker

5) England beat Switzerland 6-5 on penalties to secure a win in the third place play-off, who was the unlikely scorer of England's fifth penalty in the shoot-out?

Jordan Pickford

Managers – Answers

1) Which match was the last that Kevin Keegan managed the England team?
England 0-1 Germany, the last game at the old Wembley Stadium in 2000

2) Who was caretaker manager for England's 0-0 draw away to Finland in October 2000?
Howard Wilkinson

3) Which manager was the first to hand David Beckham the captaincy of England, doing so in a friendly versus Italy in 2000?
Peter Taylor

4) How many major Quarter-Finals did Sven-Goran Eriksson lead England to?
Three

5) Who was England manager when they drew 1-1 with Brazil in the first game at the new Wembley Stadium in June 2007?
Steve McClaren

6) Fabio Capello left his role as England manager in 2012, with his final game being a 1-0 win over who in November 2011?
Sweden

7) Who took charge of England for their 3-2 friendly defeat to the Netherlands in February 2012?
Stuart Pearce

8) Who did Roy Hodgson make permanent captain of England shortly after he took control as manager?
Steven Gerrard

9) Sam Allardyce famously only managed England for one match, a late win against which team?
Slovakia

10) Gareth Southgate faced Germany in his first match after being confirmed as permanent England manager in 2017, but who captained the side that day?
Gary Cahill

11) Which manager had taken charge of England on the most occasions this century?
Sven-Goran Eriksson (67 matches)

If you enjoyed this book please consider leaving a five star review on Amazon

Books by Jack Pearson available on Amazon:

Cricket:

Cricket World Cup 2019 Quiz Book
The Ashes 2019 Cricket Quiz Book
The Ashes 2010-2019 Quiz Book
The Ashes 2005 Quiz Book
The Indian Premier League Quiz Book

Football:

The Quiz Book of Arsenal Football Club in the 21st Century
The Quiz Book of Aston Villa Football Club in the 21st Century
The Quiz Book of Chelsea Football Club in the 21st Century
The Quiz Book of Everton Football Club in the 21st Century

The Quiz Book of Leicester City Football Club in the 21st Century

The Quiz Book of Liverpool Football Club in the 21st Century

The Quiz Book of Manchester City Football Club in the 21st Century

The Quiz Book of Manchester United Football Club in the 21st Century

The Quiz Book of Newcastle United Football Club in the 21st Century

The Quiz Book of Southampton Football Club in the 21st Century

The Quiz Book of Sunderland Association Football Club in the 21st Century

The Quiz Book of Tottenham Hotspur Football Club in the 21st Century

The Quiz Book of West Ham United Football Club in the 21st Century

The Quiz Book of the England Football Team in the 21st Century

Printed in Great Britain
by Amazon

45751778R00063